THE GIANT Book of CARTOONS AND JOKES

JOLLY GIANT

FUN FOR ALL THE FAMILY
LARGE OR SMALL

"A fine time YOU'VE picked ta run outa sticking plaster!"

"Ignore him — he's probably drunk!"

"It don't even tell ya how ta hash up a mess o' beans!"

"That could ha' been mighty serious — they might have spilled ya whusky!"

"The Smith and Wesson thirty-eight, I think."

Small boy sitting in maternity waiting room: 'I was born at six o'clock in the morning.'

Father: 'How on earth could you know that?'

Boy: 'I had to get up to switch the alarm off.'

Patient: 'Doctor, you must help me. I'm suffering from amnesia.'
Doctor: 'Go home and forget about it.'

"O.K., you got a deal —
three wishes it is, then!"

"Oh yes, the glass slipper fitted
all right, but when I kissed
him he turned into a frog."

The psychiatrist said to his patient, as the young man lay on the couch, 'Now relax and just tell me all about your early life.'

The patient said, 'Well, I can't remember the names of all the girls, but . . .'

"If I give you another kiss would
you turn back into a handsome frog?"

"That's YOUR story — how do I
know you're really a prince?"

"Have you been riding in
the plate-lift again?"

"This place must be under new management
– it used to be such a nice little
teashop back in 1948."

"If you don't cough up
the protection money
– we'll wreck the joint."

Recruit: 'You can't take me in the army!'

MO: 'And why not?'

'I've got one leg shorter than the other.'

'Don't worry. The ground won't be level where you're fighting.'

Two inmates from the local asylum, two miles away, came to gather windfalls from the local apple orchard. They filled two large sacks and a man said, 'You've got a pretty heavy load there.'

'That's right,' they told him, 'we'll change half-way.'

"You'd better put your shirt on quick! That's the Admiral's wife!"

"I said I'm sorry — what more do you want?"

"Crow's nest to bridge — the fog's clearing, and we should be seeing the old white cliffs of Dover any time now."

"On my shoulder, stupid!"

"Not fish AGAIN!"

'What are my chances of recovering, doctor?' asked the patient.

'One hundred percent,' said the doctor. 'Medical records prove that nine out of ten people die of the disease you have. Yours is the tenth case I've treated and all the others died. So you see, you're bound to get well.'

"Anything else, sir? Confetti? Lucky horseshoes?"

A doctor got a frantic call from a housewife: 'Doctor, come quickly!' she said. 'It's my husband. When he got up this morning he took his vitamin pill, his tranquilliser, his antihistamine pill, his appetite depressant pill and he added just a little dash of benzedrine. Then he lit a cigarette and there was this tremendous explosion!'

A fellow went to visit his doctor for a general check up. After he'd finished examining him the doctor said: 'Tell me, what are all those tiny little pinpricks all over your chest?'

'Oh, those?' he said. 'Well, you see, I spend a lot of time in a nudist colony and last week it was Poppy Day!'

'Are your eyes improving?'

'Sure they are, sir.'

'Can you see better? Can you see the nurse now?'

'Sure oi can, sir! She gets plainer and plainer every day!'

Attractive patient: 'They tell me, doctor, that you're a real lady killer.'

Doctor: 'Oh, no! I assure you, I make no distinction between the sexes.'

"There must be a stack of them behind that hill — one drops behind there every night."

"I like them myself — mind you, I wouldn't let my daughter marry one."

The doctor put the extremely fat woman on a diet. She was so fat that standing up she looked like she was sitting down! The doctor said to her, 'You can have three lettuce leaves, one piece of dry toast, a glass of orange juice and one tomato.'

'Do I take them before or after meals, doctor?'

"Smashing new secretary — look at her biceps!"

"How many times do I have to tell you not to be cruel to helpless creatures?"

Did you hear about the Chef who always suffered from insomnia and lay in bed counting shepherd's pies?

"We've got to stop meeting like this, girls — my wives are getting suspicious."

"We must organise a proper sandpit for them."

"Loitering, eh?"

The man called at the doctor's and said: 'Could you possibly give me six bottles of medicine for my wife?'

'*Six* bottles for your wife?' he asked. 'What's wrong with her?'

'Well, doctor,' he said, 'I don't know really. There isn't anything wrong with her but my friend told me that after one bottle of your medicine his wife was a different woman and I thought I'd get six bottles to make sure.'

"I had a parrot once but it bit me!"

'I insisted on the nurse being present while the doctor was examining me this afternoon,' the woman told her friend.

'Heavens! Couldn't you trust him alone?' she asked.

'Of course,' she said, 'but I couldn't trust her alone in the waiting room with my husband.'

"How do yer keep yer feet so soft and white, mate?"

"They say that if you hold one to your ear, you can hear the washing machines!"

A doctor hoping to cure a man of his alcoholism asked him: 'How did you come to get so completely intoxicated?'

'I got into bad company, doctor,' he said. 'You see, there were four of us, I had a bottle of whisky and the other three were tee-totallers.'

"I DID speak to him, dearest, but he didn't answer."

"I always said they were a couple of big-heads!"

"It's the neighbours again, complaining about the noise from our radio."

"I think we had better let him have his lawn mower back!"

"And by just giving that knob half a turn to the right, we can blast the neighbours out of bed!"

A doctor diagnosed a patient's condition as too much worrying over money matters. 'Relax,' he ordered. 'Just two weeks ago I had another fellow here and he couldn't pay his tailor's bills, so I told him to forget about them and now he feels great.'

'I know,' said the patient, 'I'm his tailor.'

"Really, Mr. Mason! What if your wife were to come out?"

"Don't ask Dad to help — it will only remind him of his lost licence!"

The doctor looked at the child's chart in the hospital which read: 'Child vomited a great deal at 5 pm. Father coming up later.'

Doctor: 'Did that medicine I gave to your uncle straighten him out?'
   Man: 'Yes, they buried him last week.'

A chap was sitting in the doctor's waiting room, reading a newspaper. He turned to a fellow sitting next to him and said: 'It's a shame about the Titanic, isn't it?'

"Let's face it, J.B. . . . Our idea of an office party may not be everybody's!"

"We thought this model would be more in keeping with the spirit of Christmas."

A man took his wife to the doctor and showed the doctor his wife's hands. 'Look, doctor, she did it while preparing my meal. It's frost-bite.'

Doctor: 'Hello, Mr James. Why is the right side of your face in a bandage?'
   Mr James: 'Because my wife is left-handed.'

"How many more wretched threepenny bits are there in this Christmas pudding?"

'Jim will be in hospital for a long time,' said the man to his friend's wife.

'Why, have you seen the doctor?' she asked.

'No,' he replied, 'but I've seen the nurse.'

"Hold it!"

The woman certainly needed to visit a plastic surgeon! Her face was so wrinkled, she didn't dare wear long earrings — made her look like a venetian blind.

"You're standing on my husband!"

The queue in the doctor's waiting room always moves very, very slowly. He's even got his stethoscope on a party line!

"This is something in the nature of a brand new venture for the social club, sir."

The warden was making his usual round at the asylum and saw one of the inmates sitting on a small stool holding a fishing rod. He had the end of the rod dangling in the wash basin. Trying to be kind the warden asked: 'Catch anything?'

The inmate replied: 'In a wash basin? Are you crazy?'

"Angela! Just hand the olives around in HERE."

"Oh, you ARE lucky! — I wish I had some poor relations!"

"Would you care to wait in the library, sir? It's down the road next to the Town Hall."

" . . . and a dash of soda on the starboard whisker, James!"

A doctor stammered rather badly. One day a man rushed into his surgery and said: 'Here's my X-rays which they gave me at the hospital. They say you're to look at them and phone me later. I still have the pains, mostly in the back now though. Oh, and would you make out a prescription for those same pills again, I'll call back tomorrow.'

With that he slammed the door and went out. The doctor said: 'C-c-c-c-come in!'

"Will that be all, sir?"

"And enter our surprise guest for the evening
— with her inimitable patter — MISSUS BLOGGS!"

"Rover's certainly taken a fancy to your after-shave lotion!"

Some doctors should be more careful. One of them, who didn't know my uncle was a cement mixer, told him that he should lose himself in his work. My uncle is now a left turn on the M1.

"Don't be silly, of course you're not keeping us up."

PHILHANSON

"They DID say Thursday, didn't they?"

DICKENS

"We sat at home all evening wondering who we should visit, and you won . . . "

" . . . I'll say this for Edna — I can bring the boys home for supper at any hour and she'll always rustle up something . . . "

"You can't give up now . . . you're nearly out of Dover Harbour!"

"Missed it again!"

"Oh no!"

A woman had been visiting a Harley Street plastic surgeon for ages. Then she read *Exodus* and was so impressed that she had her nose changed back.

"Don't look now, but isn't that our new goalkeeper?"

"Wouldn't you prefer to read something, sir?"

"Miss Greenslade, will . . . will you marry me?"

"I don't get it, nurse — he didn't give ME any trouble taking his medicine."

"First thing to do is loosen the patients clothing."

"Hello? Pardon? Speak up!"

There's the story of a peasant from a European country, who had to go to hospital for an operation. As soon as he arrived there he was given a really good bath. As he left the bathroom he remarked to a nurse: 'Well, it wasn't as bad as I expected. I've been dreading that operation for years!'

He went to the doctor and said, 'I've got a terrible pain, doc.'

The doctor said, 'Tell me, do you have any trouble passing water?'

'Well, I do get a little giddy when I go over a bridge.'

"What do you mean, you can't find the starter?"

"Why ever did you invite your twin sister round? — You know I hate the sight of her!"

"I've been eating my lunch this way for thirty years — you'll have to be patient, now that I'm retired!"

"When is Mum coming home with our new baby, Dad?"

A young girl came out of the doctor's surgery, crying her eyes out. Another patient asked the doctor what the matter was and the doctor said: 'I told the young lady that she was expecting a happy event.'

The patient asked, 'Well, is she?'

He said: 'No, but it's cured her hiccups.'

The pretty young girl was a nurse, but she had to give it up. She didn't like the arrangements at the wealthy house where she worked – the kids were too backward and the father too forward.

" . . . and this is where the Duchess and I sleep."

"You rang, sir?"

The professor was discussing anatomy with medical students and he finished by saying: 'The human body is an interesting phenomenon. Often a pat on the back will result in a swollen head.'

"I keep meaning to phone the taxidermist about that!"

"Am I right in assuming this is your first plain-clothes assignment, Constable?"

"Once upon a time . . ."

"Up to now, Higgins, we've been pretty lenient . . ."

"Never been the same since 'e took the dog-handling course!"

A doctor somersaulted his car twice. Incredibly, alive and unscathed, he staggered to a nearby cottage where he knew he could phone the garage. The lady of the house was just replacing the phone. 'Oh, doctor, I've only just called your house,' she said. 'How good of you to come so quickly. There's been a terrible accident outside.'

" . . . and furthermore, madam, impersonating an officer."

"Hullo! Ron? You asked me to phone if ever I found myself at a loose end one evening."

Hear about the new contraceptive pill for Catholics? It weighs three tons. You simply put it up against the bedroom door and the husband can't get in.

"Sorry, Ben, but I just can't go steady with you any longer — I've got a crick in the neck!"

"Why, Ralph, I DO believe you're jealous!"

"I'm glad he's not just after my money!"

The expectant father paced the corridor of the maternity hospital. He was extremely agitated, wanting the event to happen as soon as possible and hoping desperately for a son. At last the doctor appeared. 'Tell me, what is it – a boy or a girl?' the man asked.

'Tr-tr-tr-,' the doctor stammered.

The man said, 'Triplets?'

'Qu-qu-qu-,' spluttered the doctor.

The man paled: 'Quadruplets,' he moaned.

'N-n-n-no,' the doctor shouted. 'Qu-qu-qu-quite the c-c-contrary. Tr-tr-try to t-t-take it quietly – it's a girl '

" 'COURSE I'll be home by midnight, Mum — I'll have cleaned John out long before then!"

"I think it was suicide."

"Excuse me, sir, are you a lover?"

"Why, Herb Trimble! What brings YOU out on a night like this?"

The doctor told his patient that drinking milk in bed was bad for him.

'In what way?' he asked.

'Simple,' said the doctor. 'You drink milk. You toss and turn in your sleep, the milk is turned to butter, the butter turns to fat, fat turns to alcohol — and you wake up with a hangover!'

nobody is to leave this room!"

"Would you like to ask Bonnie to tune it down a bit, Clyde?"

Did you hear about the nervous surgeon who was finally discharged from the hospital; It wasn't so much all the patients he lost, it was those deep gashes he made in the operating table.

'Remember,' the doctor said to the middle-aged man, 'it may be true that life begins at forty, but after fifty it's only from the waist up!'

"So ends my first day as children's nursemaid at the Grange. Something tells me this is not a happy house."

Two small boys were wandering around the medical college. One of them saw a skeleton on view and said to his friend: 'Bet you don't know what a skeleton is?'

'Of course I do!' he shouted. 'It's bones with the people off!'

"Dammit! If the A.A won't come, phone the R.A.C.!"

'I can't sleep at night. The least little sound disturbs me; I'm the victim of insomnia. Even the cat on the back fence wakes me up at night.'

'This powder will be very effective, sir.'

'When do I take it?'

'You don't. Give it to the cat in milk.'

"That's a rotten lie! We were just good friends!"

A man who smoked one hundred cigarettes a day, went to see his doctor because he was suffering from a sore throat. The poor man could hardly speak above a whisper. Pointing to his throat he said hoarsely: 'Cigarettes.'

The doctor said: 'Smoking them?'

He said, 'No, asking for them.'

"Do you mind if I smoke?"

An old boozer went to see his doctor with a bad attack of the shakes. The doctor took one look at him and said: 'Drunk again!'

The old boozer said: 'OK doc, I'll come back when you're sober!'

"All right, Johnson, for the last time — what have you done with the light bulbs?"

Last year, Americans spent more than eighteen billion dollars on medical care. And it's really doing the job. More and more doctors are getting well!

"D'you mind — I'm trying to sleep!"

CLEW

"I'm not that sort of a girl!
I'm not that sort of a girl!"

"Sorry it cost you six pounds
taking me out . . . leave your
address and I'll post it on to you!"

"Boy is he loaded! Last night
his wallet fell on my foot!"

A young medical student was
having a very difficult time with
his examination. It contained
many questions that were far too
difficult for him to answer. He
was asked: 'How would you
induce a copious perspiration?'
He wrote: 'I would get the patient
to take the medical examination at
this college.'

"An' when a politician gets elected,
what does 'e do? I'll tell you.
Nothing, mate, exactly NOTHING!"

"You owe me for ten pintas, two poundas,
and three dozenas. I'll be glad if you'd
pay off parta if not alla!"

"Yer said I could work stripped
to the waist didn't yer?"

"I do quite a trade with the office-staff."

"Can't wait for a lovely cuppa
when we've finished, eh, Mike?"

Proud father telegramming
his mother: 'Gladys had
triplets. Doing well. More
tomorrow.'

One germ said to another:
'Stay away from me, Cyril.
I've got a touch of
penicillins.'

A party of visitors were being shown over a large asylum. They passed in front of a large cell in which a man sat, nursing a large doll, which was dressed in the costume of an up-to-date young lady.

'That man,' said the doctor, 'has a very sad history. He spends most of his time fondling that doll. You see, he was once engaged to a girl, whom he loved and she jilted him and got married to another man. He lost his reason over the affair.'

The visitors were very touched and passed to the next cell. 'And this,' said the doctor, 'is the other man.'

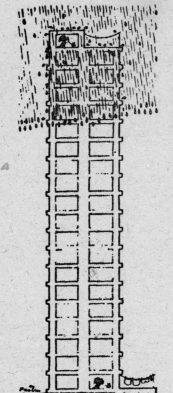

"Oi, Mary! Rain on the way!"

The spinal column is a bunch of bones that run up your back keeping you from being legs all the way up.

"So THAT was the noise I heard last night!"

'Tell me honestly doctor, how do I stand?'
    'I don't know, that's what puzzles me.'

'Is the doctor in?'
    'He's practising at the moment.'
    'OK. I'll come back when he's perfect.'

"Hold it, Frilby! You'll swoop when I tell you to swoop!"

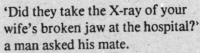

'Did they take the X-ray of your wife's broken jaw at the hospital?' a man asked his mate.

'Well, they tried to,' he replied, 'but they got a moving picture.'

"All the book says is 'No smoking and no drinking whilst on duty'"

"Is this man pestering you, Miss?"

'Gee, I'm tired! I was up all last night with a sick friend.'

'Who was he?'

'I don't know he was too sick to tell me!'

A Polish man went to the eye hospital for an eye test. Seated in front of the chart, the doctor asked him to read through the lines one at a time. As the man got to the botton line, which read CSVENCZW, he hesitated. The doctor said, 'Don't look so worried, if you can't read it just try your best.'

The Polishman said: 'Read it? I *know* the fellow personally!'

"And you are requested to make no attempt to leave the neighbourhood until our inquiries are completed."

"Grandma's ill. We'll have to try to manage without her!"

"Well, I just hope we understand who's boss now!"

When a doctor X-rays the lungs of a dog, what do you think he finds? The seat of his trousers!

'Doctor, what would you give me for a sore throat?' 'Nothing, I don't want one.'

The expectant father was pacing the floor and said to another anxious father-to-be: 'I'm going to have a big party to celebrate the arrival of our new baby.'

The other father-to-be said, 'Great. I'll bring the cigars.'

'Oh, no. No kid of mine is going to smoke.'

"It's scared stiff of flies, but it does keep the relations away."

"Boy! I'd hate to be you if anyone finds out about this!"

"It's nice to eat out for a change."

"Just you squeak when you're spoken to!"

"I was hoping we would be alone tonight."

"You're all right, Sir, but I'm afraid we will have to take the horse away for further tests!"

"That looks suspicious — the Mint with a hole in it."

POLICE DOGS TRAINING CENTRE

"I like the idea of giving them a sporting chance."

A man had a reputation as a road hog. He was lying in a hospital bed after an accident. The doctor asked the nurse: 'How is he this morning?'

She said: 'Oh, he keeps putting his right hand out!'

'Ah,' said the doctor, 'he's turning the corner!'

"Watch out, he's a proper Casanova! Dammit, he's even made a pass at ME!"

" . . . and I can assure you that the strength of our product is exceptional . . . "

"Good morning, Miss Bennet — take a letter!"

"Did you HAVE to duplicate and circulate that note I'd slipped in about our weekend at Brighton?"

"My typxwritxr's gonx wring."

'What's this bump on your head?'
'It's from my tonsil operation.'
'How on earth could you get a bump on your head from a tonsil operation?'
'They ran out of ether!'

"Mr. Henderson, you're wanted on the phone."

"He's generally in a good mood between his mid-morning depression and after-lunch hangover, if you can find it!"

First man: 'Call me a doctor — call me a doctor!'

Second man: 'What's the matter? Are you sick?'

First man: 'No, I've just graduated from medical school!'

Doctor: 'Afraid you're going to have insomnia? What are the symptoms?'

Woman: 'Twins!'

"Wake up, dear — we're at the station."

"Just remember that I'M the head of this company!"

"Managing Director or not, if you WILL come to the office so early . . . "

"Catch ME wearing a see-through blouse!"

A hospital patient had two charts over his bed: one showing how he was getting along with his treatment and another showing how he was getting along with his nurse!

She rushed off to the hospital to prevent them from operating on her boy friend. She didn't want anyone else opening her male!

"O.K., so it can be done — but what does it prove?"

"Have a chat with that little blonde widow in the spotted dress, George. She's probably lonely."

"O.K.! Who's the comedian who dumped all the empties around mother?"

The stout gentleman went to see his doctor and told him that he was suffering with stomach trouble. 'What sort of trouble?' the doctor asked him.

He said, 'I can't get my trousers over it.'

"Don't be silly, Gladys — your parties are ALWAYS lovely!"

The chemist danced with joy around the shop till the bottles rattled! 'What's wrong?' asked the assistant, 'are you ill?'

'No,' he said. 'But do you remember when our water pipes were frozen last winter?'

'Yes, but what has that . . .'

'Well, the plumber who fixed them has just come in to have a prescription filled!'

"Don't underestimate us, Millbright. We have ways of teaching you to talk."

"The formula from a top Civil Servant is in our hands!
'First warm the pot . . . "

The doctor was examining his patient. 'You smoke far too much,' he advised.

'Yes, doctor,' said the patient, 'so my wife tells me. In fact she absolutely assured me that if I die she'll bury my pipe and box of matches with me.'

'You may not require the matches.'

A motorist stopped by the police for speeding, said he had an appointment with his dentist. It sounds like a *very* improbable story.

"Just now and again, Mr. Easel, do you think I might have the rent in cash?"

The psychiatrist said to the middle-aged patient: 'Tell me, have you had any dreams lately?'

'No, I haven't doc.'

'Hard luck,' said the psychiatrist. 'I've had some corkers.'

Patient to psychiatrist: 'Furthermore, my wife doesn't understand me, doc.'

'In what way?'

'Well, the other day I was sitting in my bath when she walked straight in and with one swipe she sank my plastic duck.'

"Did I ever tell you about my operation, dear?"

"Henry — bath's ready!"

"What's all this then — the wife changed her bath night?"

"I'll be glad when our landlord mends the bath!"

"I see you've fixed the car"

A psychologist is a man you pay to ask questions your wife asks you for nothing.

A dentist was suspected of having beaten his wife to death with an iron bar. No doubt he won her confidence by assuring her that it wouldn't hurt a bit.

The poor psychiatrist wasted a **whole** hour talking to a man on his couch before he found out that the fellow **was** re-upholstering it.

Mr Isaac Greenbaum is making **a fortune** in Harley Street. According to his press agent he's selling advertising space **on** psychiatrist's ceilings.

"I'll NEVER get the cleaning done at this rate, sir!"

"Sorry, Miss Carter . . . I should have warned you about the electric fire behind that screen!"

Did you hear about the lady chiropodist who married a dentist? They fought tooth and nail.

An elephant went to a psychiatrist **and asked** for help. The doctor said, 'What's the problem?'
The elephant shrugged and said, 'Amnesia.

A man was so upset over recent events that it affected him very much indeed, and he went to see his psychiatrist. It seems that the man had had three wives. And they all died in the past two years or so. The doctor said: 'Tell me about it.'

'Well, the first one ate poisoned mushrooms. The second one also ate poisoned mushrooms, and the third one cracked her skull.'

The psychiatrist said: 'How is that?'

'She wouldn't eat the poisoned mushrooms.'

"How long have you had this fear of heights?"

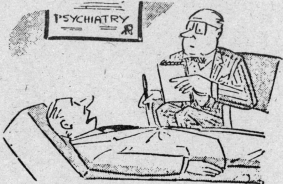

"I don't MIND being a Hot-Dog, but the mustard ruins my clothes . . ."

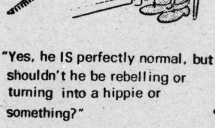

"Yes, he IS perfectly normal, but shouldn't he be rebelling or turning into a hippie or something?"

A famous dentist announced that the Eskimos enjoy pain. Mind you, dentists have that idea about everybody.

"Now tell me, when you lose your temper, do you go to extremes?"

Remember. Never argue with a doctor. He has inside information.

Cannibal to cannibal doctor: 'I don't like the look of my wife.'

Doctor: 'Never mind, just eat the potatoes.'

Hear about the expectant filmstar father in the maternity hospital? He wanted to name his baby Oscar because it was his best performance of the year.

"Ethel, where did you buy this new linen basket?"

Small boy: 'Dad! There's a doctor at the front door with a moustache.'

Father: 'Tell him I've got one.'

Hear about the Harley Street plastic surgeon who dozed off in front of the fire? He melted.

A fine looking, athletic man was attending an examination prior to going into the navy. The doctor had given him a thorough going over and seemed very pleased. The recruit said, 'I must go and tell my wife; she's waiting in the next room.'

The doctor frowned and said: 'Er – not that large horsey woman with the straight hair, four chins and buck teeth?'

'That's her!' said the young man.

The doctor said: 'I'm afraid you'll be rejected my good man, you'd never pass the eye test!'

Those new miracle drugs I've been reading about in the medical journal sound so good I'm sorry I'm healthy.

A chap had just bought contact lenses at the opticians, and a friend of his met him outside and said: 'Yes, they're all right, I guess, but what do you put on in case a fight starts?'

"You're going to look a right nit if it don't snow."

" . . . and you call yourself a plumber!"

"And I tell you Sir Walter Raleigh used his OWN coat."

"Brilliant forecasting, Woppleton, the Met Office is proud of you!"

John had been sent to see the firm's doctor. 'How did you get on, John?' asked his employer.

'All right, sir, but I didn't go to your doctor – he had 10 to 1 on his brass plate. The doctor opposite had 9 to 5 on his so I went to 'im – the odds were much better!'

"Yoo, hoo, dear! What's for supper?"

'I'm afraid old Brown won't live very long. He has one foot in the grate.'

'Don't you mean one foot in the grave?'

'No, he's going to be cremated.'

"Don't panic! His brain is only as big as a hen's egg."

'It must be wonderful to be a doctor,' mused the young man. 'I mean, in what other job could you ask a girl to take all her clothes off, look at her at leisure, and then maybe send the husband the bill?'

"Go home, Spot."

"My grandfather told me that before the nuclear war he had to get down on his knees and propose before he could get one of these!"

"A room with a bath, please."

She's got 15 children. She's stork-raving mad.

"I'm checking on reports that you're sub-letting your council house, Mrs. Moxon."

'There seems to be very little sickness in your village,' said a visitor to a resident. 'Yes,' the resident replied. 'We've only one doctor, you know, and he is very unpopular.'

"I told you they were very strict here about guests being prompt for meals!"

The anxious husband went to see a doctor who had been treating his wife. 'My wife doesn't seem to be progressing, doctor,' he told him.

'No,' answered the doctor, 'When she gains a little strength, she uses it all up trying to tell her friends what's the matter with her!'

"That's my husband – he's an art student like yourself."

"That's funny — you're the third 'arold Wilson I've booked this afternoon."

"Can't I forget about strategy and just fight for my life?"

FOLEY

"You're in luck! I've managed to fix you up with a return fight!"

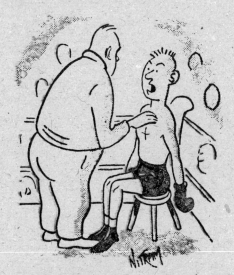

"I'll wear my teeth this round — he's biting."

REX

"It ain't against the law to hit him back, yer know."

She: 'It's really marvellous how much that doctor knows.'

He: 'Why?'

She: 'He asked me if I ever had a buzzing in my ears.'

He: 'Well?'

She: 'That's just where I *do* hear it!'

"I didn't get no 'at in me cracker!"

There was the story of the surgeon who, frankly, drank far too much for his own good. One day he turned up at the operating theatre and told the nurse: 'It's all right to wheel the patient out now, nurse.'

'But doctor,' she said, 'we haven't wheeled him in yet!'

'Indeed!' declared the surgeon. 'Then what have I been doing for the past fifteen minutes?'

'I *know* what you've been doing,' she replied. 'You have amputated the leg of the operating table!'

An Irishman with one eye called Murphy — no one knows what the other eye was called — called on his doctor and the doctor said: 'Murphy, have you 'flu?'

He said, 'No, doc, I've come on me scooter.'

"No thanks! I bought him a hedge-trimmer LAST year — and there was nothing left of the Christmas tree by Boxing Day!"

"Is it REALLY necessary for our cat to send one to Wilson's cat?"

Doctor: 'Considering the weak state of your eyes, I would suggest it would be good for you to gaze into empty space.'

Patient: 'Thank you, doc. I'll keep looking into my wallet.'

"What d'you mean, 'Get on the couch'? – I AM a couch!"

Kelly

Patient: 'How can I ever repay you for your kindness to me?'
Doctor: 'By cheque, postal order or cash.'

'I'm in a marvellous new hospital,' she told her friend.
'I get everything I want. They even have non-stick bed pans.'

D Colman

"I'm told you've got an inferiority complex."

"Isn,t it amazing? That psychiatrist certainly cured our Myrtle's claustrophobia"

"See a psychiatrist? – I AM a psychiatrist!"

A terrible accident happened at the racecourse at Brighton last week. One of the judges fell and broke his leg and the vet shot him!

A lady being operated on for appendicitis asked her doctor if the scar would show. He said: 'It ought not to!'

"Is it okay if he pays cash, Mr. Wilkins?"

"If she tells us how she was walled up in 1358 just once more I shall SCREAM!"

"They keep very much to themselves. Occasionally they drop in on a Sunday to watch the Epilogue."

"Oh, don t apologise for mistaking this for the bank — my wife always does . . ."

"Quick! Where's your cheque book? The bank's getting some more money in."

"I see Maisie's got behind with the milk bill again!"

A health inspector was walking through the grounds of a mental asylum one sunny afternoon, when he suddenly stopped to admire a beautifully designed flower bed. He was very surprised to discover that it was the work of one of the inmates. He said to the man concerned, 'You're obviously cured! I shall speak to the governor right away about your discharge from here and arrange a job for you in the parks department, I promise you.'

As the inspector approached the governor's house he was a hit by a brick — wielded by the gardener inmate. The inmate grinned, 'Now, please, don't forget your promise, will you?'

The health official was showing a party of visitors around the mental hospital and as they walked through the gate they heard a loud noise coming from behind the wall that surrounded the asylum. In the shadow of the bushes a young man was attacking the wall with a heavy hammer and a crowbar. The official left the party and said to the man, 'What on earth are you doing?'

'Hush!' came the reply, 'can't you see I'm trying to break out of here?' and he resumed his slamming of the wall.

'Look,' said the official, 'there's a gate just across there.'

The inmate grinned knowingly, 'I know that,' he admitted 'but it squeaks.'

"Taxi!"

"We'll have to stop seeing each other
. . . my wife's getting wise to what
happened to the Foreign Legion."

"Some people have no shame,
forever cadging lifts."

"If you're thinking of asking her
for the next dance — forget it!"

"Trust them to come today with our front room all of a mess with the paperhanging . . ."

"I've phoned the Air Ministry, and they say there's a perfectly logical explanation . . ."

"Now THERE'S a sight you don't see very often."

Patient: 'Doctor, what I need is something to stir me up, and to put me in fighting form. Have you got anything like that in a prescription?'

Doctor: 'No! You'll find it in my bill.'

The nurse notified the hospital visitor: 'Your mother-in-law needs a blood transfusion but we can't find the blood to match her's.'

The visitor asked: 'Have you tried a baboon?'

"Does that 'Forsaking all others' include the Queen's Head Darts Team?"

"Dad! Uncle Bert! At last we've got someone to do the washing up!"

" 'Let him now speak, or forever hold his peace!' Was that loud enough?"

REX

"How do I know it will cause controversy? Because today's Monday."

"And now you have forty seconds to throw all these balloons into the air and catch them in the net fixed to this scooter!"

"Do you have visiting hours?"

"Normal lines of communication have broken down, but our man has got a message through . . . ."

"The Prime Minister has assured us that there is no need for alarm."

"The little darling
wants to go flysies."

"Just as I thought! Selling your
soul to the devil as soon as my
back is turned!"

"I'm fed up with being the lesser of two evils!"

"This is my brother Joe. Good lad,
really — but he just couldn't lay off
the women!"

"You strike a hard bargain, Madam,
but I agree — Eternal Youth AND
a million stamps!"

A very disturbed man sought his analyst and said, 'I have developed a phobia that is really ruining my work. Crowds make me violently sick.'

'What's your business?' asked the doctor.

The patient said, 'I'm a pick-pocket.'

"It's a pity you haven't got an INFERIORITY complex. I'm rather good at those."

"You're not giving me enough time. Can't you put off your march on Moscow till next week?"

A woman considered going to a Harley Street surgeon to get a face lift, in fact everything lifted! Particularly her nose. It was *very* big. If she wore a veil, from the back it looked as though she was trawling for mackerel. From the front it looked as though she'd caught one.

"Why do you want to see a psychiatrist? I like you just as you are, dear — kind, easy-going, stupid."

"He's fine until we get into the park, doctor."

"Ah'd like ta purchase three 'Git-well' cards."

A woman took her youngest to the doctors. During the examination the doctor commented, 'Well, at least you could have washed his neck.'

The woman said, 'I did.'

Then the doctor took a piece of cotton wool, dipped it in spirit, stroked it across the boy's neck and pointed out the clear stripe. 'See?' he said.

'Well,' she said slowly, 'if you're going to dry clean him . . .'

"Aw, stop makin' setch a fuss — anybody'd think I wuz pulling a tooth out, stead o' jest a li'l ole bullet."

". . . then Red Ridin' Hood reached for her six-gun an' said 'O.K. Grandma make yore play'!"

"Last owner wuz a dame."

There was a dear old maid who went to see a specialist. For half an hour the specialist rubbed, massaged and manipulated her stomach and then said: 'How's that then?'

The old maid looked up at him and said: 'That's fine, doctor, but the pain I came to see you about is in my left foot.'

Patient: 'Doc! I've just swallowed
a tin of gold paint!'
   Doctor: 'How do you feel?'
   Patient: 'Guilty!'

Moss

"Actually, His Excellency seems
quite friendly, I think it's
the interpreter who doesn't like us."

" 'Let's go into exile' you said,
in a few weeks they'll be
begging us to come back', you said . . ."

We pledge you our support to the end!

"Say hallo to the nice, paleface, children."

An asylum superintendent saw an inmate writing a letter. 'Who are you writing to?' he asked.

'I'm writing to myself,' came the reply.

'And what are you writing to yourself?' he queried.

'How the hell should I know!' shouted the inmate. 'I shan't get this letter till tomorrow.'

"Blacklegs!"

"I'm giving you 24 hours to git outa town."

"Tumbleweed sure plays his part in openin' up the West."

"Must it have a moat?"

"I thought there was a catch in it somewhere — you don't see many bungalows at that price!"

Doctor: 'Put your tongue out. Out! Come on, all of it!'
    Child: 'I can't, doctor — it's fastened at the other end.'

"Hw. Did yu Knw. I ws. an Este. Agt?"

"We'd like something near a school."

"Phew! That was a bit tight — I didn't think we were going to make it."

ROY NIXON

KLUTCH'S SCHOOL OF MOTORING

"Right hand down a bit, Mr Sibthorpe!"

STAFFORDSHIRE

"D'yer have to make it so obvious that this is our first car?"

"What'll it be, podner? Regular, Highgrade or Supergallop?"

"Ah say, do away wi' shot-guns fust

"Ah never did care much fer discussion groups."

"Naw, stranger, he ain't daid drunk — jest daid."

A physician ran into trouble with a patient who had obviously been over-eating. He advised: 'Just cut out all starches and sweets and smoke one cigar a day.'

At the end of the fortnight he was back at the surgery looking really awful. 'I cut out all the starches and sweets,' he remarked, 'but that one cigar a day nearly killed me – I've never smoked before in my life.'

"If I thought for a moment that you were smiling!"

"Henry, fetch your hacksaw and make it up with mother."

" . . . about this letter you sent us in 1950, saying you were coming for a week . . . "

"Sorry, mother, I forgot about your headache!"

"Traffic lights ahead, dear . . . better get landing permission!"

"Kindly stand clear, sir, while I release the bonnet."

"It fills me with 'orror, Bert — 'aving to stand by an' watch all that lovely beer go flat!"

"I'll never come home drunk, I might see two of you."

"I never drink and drive — I find it slops all over the steering — wheel."

'Doctor, my husband always talks in his sleep,' said the worried wife.

'I'll give him something that will cure him,' said the doctor.

'Oh, don't do that,' implored the wife. 'I want you to give him something that will make him more distinct.'

"He's my greatest achievement, I made him a millonaire."

"Dare you to slam the gate and ask him for his season!"

LOST PROPERTY

"About 7lb 2oz., with fair hair and blue eyes."

"Please yourself — either pay up or let go!"

LEFT LUGGAGE

A banker went to a doctor for a check up. Finally the doctor told him, 'You're as sound as a dollar.'

'As bad as that,' said the banker, and passed out.

The coroner was questioning the young doctor, who had only just qualified, and whose patient had died under tragic circumstances. The doctor told him exactly what happened: 'You see, sir,' he told him, 'this man came into me with a very bad cut in his head. The blood was pouring from it, I didn't know what to do for a moment and then I remembered my manual — so I put a tourniquet on his neck!'

"Been downstairs all night, Pa — helping a man to pack for his holidays!"

'I suppose you're getting a good fee for attending the Smythington-Johnson kid?'

'Well, yes,' said the doctor, 'a pretty good fee, but why do you ask?'

'Well, I 'ope yer won't ferget that it was my little Alfie wot threw the brick wot 'it 'im!'

"This getting up and going to work every morning, breaks up my whole day."

"Bit stingy with the chips, aren't they?"

Crazy story! A kipper – he was Jewish, his first name was Yom – a kipper went to the doctors and said: 'Is smoking bad for you?' The doctor said that it was. The kipper then said: 'Well, it cured *me*!'

"George, do you happen to have a Henry the Eighth penny on you?"

"Let's wait here. These two look like a couple of fast eaters."

'Why are you so sad?' a man was asked.
'My aunt's just died,' he said.
'But you were never very fond of her.'
'I know,' he said, 'but I was the means of keeping her in a lunatic asylum during the last five years of her life. She has left me all her money and now I've got to prove that she was of sound mind.'

"Oh, stop complaining, George! It's not Grandad's fault the donkeys aren't here this year."

'Doctor, I've got spots before my eyes, what shall I do?'
'Don't scratch them!'

"I suppose we can be thankful for one thing . . . it's eased up considerably since last week!"

'Before we discuss taking you on as an instructor here, would you kindly GET OFF MY FOOT?"

'Midships, Commander — midships!"

"Never again do I go to a firemen's dance!"

"I hear they simply WRECKED a train on the way."

A man was told by his doctor that he must stop drinking and to overcome his craving he advised him to eat something every time he felt the desire to drink come over him. The man tried it and to his surprise — it worked! One night, however, in his hotel room, he heard a strange noise in the next room and so he went to have a look through the key-hole. He saw a man about to hang himself, on a chair, from the ceiling. He rushed downstairs, three at a time, and grabbed hold of the waiter. 'L-ll-isten,' he stammered, 'there's a f-f-fella in the next room to me . . . he's hanging himself . . . for heaven's sake get me a plate of ham and eggs!'

"Now that's what I call a MAN!"

"We'll be along about eight o'clock, not seven — Desmond always takes such a time dressing."

Private Jones had been in the army for about nine months before he began to show strange signs of behaviour. One day he was found raiding a dustbin, flicking through the papers he found in there, and throwing them all over the place, shouting: 'That's not it! That's not it!' Later he was discovered going through the mess accounts. He pulled out scraps of paper, flung them away and yelled: 'That's not it! That's not it!' The redcap arrested him and took him to the CO who in turn called in the MO.

The doctor said: 'It would seem, Jones, that you are in need of treatment and this will be given to you under the Health Service in civvy street.'

As he was handed his discharge papers, which had been hastily prepared, Jones grabbed the sheet and burst into tears saying: 'This is it! This is it!'

"And now meet our judges for the military two-step,"

"None of your tricky steps, now, Freddy . . .

"Mr. Fenner — there is a buffet at the far end of the room!"

"Sorry, but I appear to be booked for the next dance."

"I've never known such a crowded dressing-room!"

"She makes lovely porridge."

"it's all relative, innit? From one point of view, I'm just a very big dwarf."

"Hold it, she's one of ours."

". . . the handsome prince turned into a juicy frog, and they had him for dinner and lived happily ever after."

"We're warning you, Guv — either that compost heap goes or we do!"

"Hey, Ali! You're praying in the wrong direction!"

"Are you quite SURE you're a qualified guide?"

"The feeling is mutual, I can assure you!"

"Guess what, mother? We're
expecting another bundle of joy!"

"I'll fix up a baby-sitter and we'll go right out and celebrate!"

"Remember asking what I did around the house all day? Well, today I DIDN'T!"

"Dinner's ready, darling, bought with my very first housekeeping money."

"Uncle Fred was a ticket clerk for over thirty years,"

"You've hit a bull, Gaffer"

"Throw us back, you fools, we're top secret!"

"Very good, sir, 480 pounds — including your wife."

"Watch it! The Guvnor's car is just coming round the corner."

"Congratulations! . . . At last a hair-spray that works in a Force Nine gale!"

"9, 10, 11 . . . seems to be one bug, missing, Professor!"

"Can I borrow a cup of type 'B' virus?"

"Is this the way to the brain drain?"

"Pass the sauce, please."

"So THAT'S what made the milkman's horse bolt!"

"You danced divinely last night, but shouldn't you have had a partner?"

"This tea tastes like strychnine!"

"Have you changed much over the years, dear?"

"Gracious, Eileen, so THAT'S why you rushed out before the end of the movie!"

"Then, after nappy-rash and windy-pops, will come your greatest trial — toothypegs . . . "

"But, Mary, I distinctly told you I wanted a BOY."

"Darling, you mean we'll soon be hearing the chatter of tiny teeth?"

"How I'd like to get married and get away from all this."

"Just think of it, Madam, no dirty
dusty corners to clean out!"

"I'm looking for a garret to starve in."

"Cosy little kitchen, isn't it?"

"To give you an idea of this neighbourhood's status, sir, that's an
abandoned car over there."

"Poke me once more, mate, and you'll see what 'Joeykins' can do."

"She's a bargain for five bob. She s going to have puppies."

"We're dead worried about it. It's right off its food."

"THAT'S not a footprint, you clot!"

"Heel!"

"Guess what, dear!"

"Blimey! You're right! It isn't Dover, it's Southend!"

"It doesn't look as though he's going to try to beat the count."

"Look — I'm sorry I said that about your mother . . "

"There must be OTHER ways of teaching him to be a good watch dog!"

"You should see her first thing in the morning."

"Blimey! That worm must be putting up a hell of a fight."

"Uh-uh! — Seems it's going to be one of those days!"

"Meet Professor Brownski, the electronics expert."

"Mrs. Bagley, you've been at my cocktail cabinet again"

"I've never met such a flippin' knowall!"

"But what are you going to DO with the world when you've taken it over?"

"Shall I be mother?"

"Women and
children first . . . . "

"Right, lads! Get the lifeboats out!"

"I'm organising a ship's concert . . . . "

"Ah, well — who's going to race who in making a nice cuppa, this bright and sunny morning?"

"Hi, gorgeous — I could lie here all day looking at your beautiful face, but I suppose you have to go and make a cup of tea, you have to . . . "

"Did you remember to lock up?"

"While you're up, Fred, get me a glass of water."

A bashful young wife was consulting a doctor. 'Do you suffer from cold feet?' he asked.

'Yes,' was the reply.

'In that case I'll give you a bottle of medicine,' the doctor told her.

'But doctor the cold feet aren't mine!'

"I think the boot put up a better fight than the tyre!"

"That's right! Go rushing off somewhere the minute your lunch is ready."

"Never mind the goldfish, fix that tap washer.

A doctor put an elderly man on a diet because of his weight problem. The man returned to his doctor in two months' time and he'd lost dozens of pounds.

The doctor was very pleased with the result.

The patient said: 'I feel so young, doctor. Only today I saw a girl's bare arm and I felt like biting it!'

The doctor said: 'You could have done. It's only about forty calories.'

"CUT!"

"Sorry I'm late, you folks."

"Oh no — YOU couldn't be content being an internationally famous film star, YOU had to make a movie."

"He told me there's no truth in the rumour that they're just good friends."

"They certainly set an example to some people during the National Anthem!"

"Here comes the head waiter Phoebe — you know, I think you SHOULD have worn a tie!"

"What's this 'Squiggle à la squiggle, twenty-five bob'?"

"On second thought, I'll have the rabbit!"

"I'll try one of those karate chops!"

"Girl? . . . What girl?"

"It's Vietnam, Cedric!"

"He's far too old for her. They say he was at Aldermaston in '63."

"Sorry! . . . I've lost the way!"

"But, Dad — YOU'RE always painting slogans around the place."

A father, who had one leg a little shorter than the other and thus walked with a slight limp, had a son who stuttered. One day the son said: 'D-d-dad, I've g-g-got a g-g-good idea, why don't you w-w-walk with one f-f-foot in the gutter? That way y-y-your limp wo-wo-wouldn't be n-n-noticed.'

'Good idea, son,' said the father, 'I'll try it.'

He did and was knocked down by a car. The son came to see him in hospital and sat by his bed and said to him: 'S-s-sorry, D-d-dad, about your accident.'

'That's all right,' he said. 'But while I've been lying here I've been thinking and I've thought of a good way of overcoming your stutter.'

'W-w-what's that, D-d-dad?' asked the son.

'Keep your bloody mouth shut!'

"Expensive? Kindly remember where you are, madam!"

NO MEANS OF SUPPORT

"Just browsing, thank you."

"You know, sometimes I wonder if it's all worth it."

WE LOVE YOU RICKY

RICK WE LOVE Y...

"Come back home, son — all is forgiven."

"Talk to me, Ethel — I can't sleep."

"I wish you'd remember to press your trousers BEFORE I get into bed."

"That is what I call a spring mattress!"

"Herbert . . . is that you creeping downstairs for a sandwich?"

"Cor! Freddie — have you seen your stars today?"

"It must be ten past three. There goes your daddy!"

"Next week, I'll sell you another casket of earth treasure!"

"I'll let my Bobby out to play with you WHEN he's done his homework!"

"Thank goodness! I'd almost given up hope!"

"This is the worst organised spontaneous demonstration, I've ever been in."

"He used to be with M.I.5"

"... then Betty and I got married, and the twins were born, so I just HAD to go commercial!"

"It's escaped!"

"I bet you can't do bird imitations."

"Good heavens, now they're checking on dog licences!"

"Mr. Smith! — You've been eating sticky toffee again."

"Do you ever wish that you could develop a severe attack of chilblains?"

"Been sent down then, have you, lad?"

"What's the score?"

"Boy! I'll be glad to get between the sheets tonight!"

"I have NOT turned communist, Saxby — I've just come off the Underground."

"Well, there definitely is NOT a body in it. You should've locked it — people'll pinch anything these days, y'know . . ."

"The jam roll going off early in your canteen is no excuse for doing seventy!"

"As a matter of fact. Mr. Pilbright, I was just on my way round to the church!"

"Didn't expect me to leave it at the reception for your relations to finish off, did you?"

"You don't mean to say you want to be cooped up inside a stuffy old church on a lovely day like this!"

ARTHUR

"A rise, Finlay? By golly, your wife hasn't wasted much time, has she!"

Kelly

"I distinctly told you — NEXT Saturday!"

"Hey, Brian! Come and take a butcher's at what we've been worshippin' for the past million years."

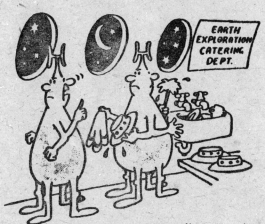

" . . . and stop throwing dirty saucers out of the window!"

"YOUR job, Fenton, is to determine whether the surface is hard or soft."

"Crikey! — I wouldn't like to meet THAT in a lonely spot on a dark night!"

"Greetings, earthman!"

"Nice to get out in the sun again, isn't it?"

"You're turning that plant into a hypochondriac!"

"This one is strictly for the enthusiast!"

"You MUST cut the lawn — what will the people on the ground floor think?"

"Sounds good – got a picture of the Captain?"

"I told you the travel allowance wouldn't last five minutes."

"Not many people know of this picnic spot."

"Shouldn't that read: 'Have you anything left'?"

"Where do I plug in the electric blanket?".

"After you've shut the window, darling, pop down and see who's ringing the door bell."

"I've just had a funny dream, Ethel!"

"I thought you were going to start some sort of new beauty treatment tonight, Sylvie."

"Mum! I just whacked a burglar! Where's Dad?"

"Nice try, Walter . . . "

"They certainly don't leave much road for cyclists!"

"By the time we get to the water with this lot on, I'll be too tired to swim."

"Well, at least we'll be able to go straight in swimming after THIS lunch!"

"Penny for the guy, mister?"

"I told you a month was too long to leave the plants!"

"I understand our new neighbours are in some kind of show business!"

"No, we don't bother with T.V. Actually my husband is thinking of buying a cinema."

"Proceeding along High Street, I observed Maggie with a male, whom I knew not to be her husband . . ."

" . . . and another thing I don't like about her — by the way, is that the sun setting or rising . . . ?"

A young married woman in London believed she was pregnant and went to the doctor to verify it. The doctor gave her a cursory examination and assured her that her suspicions were correct. Then, to her astonishment, he simply took a rubber stamp, printed something with it on her abdomen and said: 'That's all.'

The wife related this strange event to her husband and he asked: 'What does it say?'

'Well, read it,' she replied.

He found that the print was too small for him to read but a magnifying glass made everything clear. It read: 'When you can read this without a magnifying glass rush your wife to the hospital.'

"Oh, that's our next door neighbour.
Funny, she usually only comes
to borrow a cup of sugar."

"Mrs. Patterson said we'd be one
of the nicest couples in town,
if it wasn't for you."

"I'm frae downstairs — would ye mind
turning your radio up? We can
hardly hear it."

CLEW

"You'll have to speak up — my ears are full of sand."

CANINE OBEDIENCE SCHOOL

"Hundreds of cats in the pet shop and I had to pick YOU!"

A police physician was called to examine an unconscious prisoner who had been arrested and brought to the police station, for drunkenness. After a short examination the doctor said: 'This person is not suffering from the effects of alcohol, he has been drugged.'

The policeman was very disturbed and said: 'I'm thinkin' yer right, sir. I drugged him all the way to the station.'

A doctor tells about the old chap who was very sick, so sick in fact that his family was gathered at the bedside. They all tried desperately to cheer him up. 'Your colour is better,' the son said.

'Your breathing's easier,' another remarked.

'Thank goodness,' sighed the old man. 'It's nice to know I'm going to die cured.'

"Stanley could be a great pianist if he wasn't left handed!"

"Mother thinks it's time I got married and settled up."

"I wish they'd throw their crumbs on the grass instead of on the concrete."

"G-r-r-r to you, too!"

"Open wide please . . . "

Hear about the psychiatrist who had been treating a blonde for eighteen months. It cost the girl about £350 and one day she received a cheque from the psychiatrist which was seemingly a rebate for £250. He wrote: 'I don't know what's come over me, but ever since I realised your inferiority complex is incurable, I've developed a guilt complex.'

The man in the psychiatrist's office said, 'Doc, you must help me! My memory is failing me altogether. I can't remember one thing minutes after I've heard it. Sometimes I even forget my own name and it takes me all my time even to remember one thing for more than about one minute.'

The psychiatrist looked very concerned and asked kindly, 'Tell me, how long has this been going on?'

'How long has *what* been going on?'

"This is ridiculous! ALL artists use models!"

"First fine day since we've been here, so we're out making the best of it!"

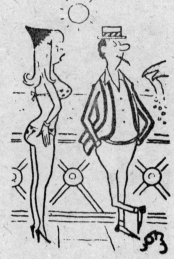

"Two weeks of the best years of my life I've given you "

"Welcome to sunny Brightsea – and please don't leave wet umbrellas, raincoats and galoshes in the bedroom."

"My husband has taken up a most unusual hobby."

"Correct me if I'm wrong, but do you advertise this place as a home from home with no restrictions, or not?"

"George, dear, it's the window cleaner!"

" . . . And if we'd gone to Spain you'd be moaning about the heat and the flies . . . !"

"back at the office. I'd be having a lovely cup of tea right now."

"Psst! I tell you he'll whip you round the cemetery, round the gas works, back to the sewage outfall and you've had it."

Some young doctors at a hospital were discussing theories about pre-natal influence.

'Obviously there's no such thing,' said one. 'It's been disproved time and time again. For instance, before I was born, my mother broke a huge pile of gramophone records but it never bothered me . . . never bothered me . . . never bothered me . . .'

In the course of his medical examination a man was asked to stretch his arms in front of him with the fingers of each hand extended. What the doctor saw was a terrific quivering and shaking in all directions. 'Good lord!' he said. 'How much do you drink?'

'Hardly any at all, doctor,' was the reply. 'I spill most of it.'

"Not that vintage! I've been saving that for a special occasion!"

"I claim sanctuary . . ."

A patient asked his doctor quite frankly what was wrong with him. 'Well,' said the doctor. 'You eat too much, drink too much and you're completely lazy.'

'Thanks,' said the patient, 'but would you be kind enough to put that into Latin then I can have a week off from the office.'

An insomniac who hadn't slept well for 32 years was on holiday in Bermuda. One morning his friend noticed that he looked more finely drawn than usual and asked him if he'd had any sleep. 'Yes, I slept,' he said, 'but I dreamed that I didn't.'

"Cut the delivery a bit fine haven't you?"

"This was my first wedding and I'm still trying to think where I went wrong!"

"Stand by your beds."

"Mr. Johnson, you're supposed
to contemplate your own navel."

"But you can't all be away the last week in August."

An overweight woman went to a doctor for help. He immediately put her on a diet and gave her a box of reducing pills with careful instructions to take no more than three a day. When she arrived home she put the box on the table while she left the room, during which time her two daughters aged three and five, found the pills and between them ate them all. The woman was naturally very worried and called the doctor, but he told her not to worry.

'They'll be nervous, wide-awake and going full steam for a couple of days,' he told her, 'but the pills won't do them any real harm, believe me.'

So for the next few days and nights the children really went wild and led the poor woman a dog's life. But the incident had one very good effect: from all the wear and tear she lost nine pounds!

When was it you sent in this
request for a raise, Simpkins?"

"Not ANOTHER of those damn industrial
espionage agents?"

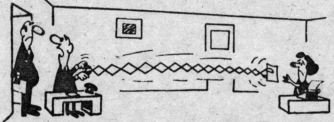

"She's got a shocking cold."

A visitor to an asylum was amazed to see
a group of ten men seated in a semi-
circle, passing half a dozen sheets of
paper back and forth to each other.
'What kind of game are they playing?' he
asked the guide. 'Is it something to do
with occupational therapy?'

'Not exactly,' was the answer. 'They're
all ex-civil servants and they're imagining
themselves back at work again.'

Danny, aged six was visiting his mother and his new
sister in the maternity hospital and getting very bored.
He wandered into the next ward to talk to an old lady
patient.

'How long have you been here?' he asked her.

'Oh, about six weeks,' she told him.

'Can I see your baby?' asked the little chap.

'I'm afraid I don't have one,' she said.

'My you're slow,' said Danny. 'My mummy's only
been here two days and she's got one already.'

"It's a terrific sensation –
I feel like a swallow!"

"Just think, Joe, if it wasn't for all that
beastly rain we could be enjoying a nice
healthy stroll down the prom.."

Just keep digging and you'll find
some yellow stuff called sand!"

"I don't think my husband trusts me."

"Rain is nature's watering can – without it,
there would be no pretty flowers, no pretty
grass, no pretty trees, no pretty . ."

"A beach to ourselves is all very well,
but I hope your friend remembers to
collect us this evening!"

Friend of the family at the maternity hospital: 'Well Charles, how do you like your new little sister?'

'Oh, she's all right,' said the little lad, 'but there are lots of other things we needed more.'

Two fathers-to-be are pacing the waiting room of the maternity hospital. Suddenly one says, 'Don't I have all the luck? This happens on my holiday.'

The other says, '*You're* complaining. This is our honeymoon.'

"I told you to observe the radar installations, comrade, not the nudists' beach!"

"We've had a warning that the room might be bugged."

"This, gentlemen, is the earliest known bugging device."

"He worked for M.I.5."

"I've been commissioned
to design a new pillar-box!"

"How's the design for the new
stamp coming along?"

A worried woman went to see her doctor and told him that her
husband appeared to have no virility and had no interest in her
whatsoever. He gave her a prescription saying: 'These will help him.
Next time you and your husband are having a quiet meal together
just slip a couple of these pills into his coffee and then come and see
me again.'

Two weeks later she went to see her doctor again and he asked her
if his remedy had been successful. 'Oh, yes, doctor,' she said,
'absolutely marvellous! I slipped the pills into my husband's coffee
and after two sips he began making love to me!'

The doctor smiled, 'Fine, no complaints then?'

She said, 'Well, there *is* one. My husband and I can't ever show
ourselves in that restaurant again.'

"Who said anything about painting?
I just want to look at you!"

" . . . and then I thought to
myself, what can I put in the
exhibition this year?"

"No, sir, Beachley Holiday Camp
is five minutes up the road!"

WORLD'S FIRST
PUNCH
AND
JUDY
STRIP
TEASE

Barry Khawkes

'I want you to look after my office while I'm away on holiday.'

'But I've only just graduated, doctor, I've had no experience.'

'That's all right, my boy. My practice is strictly fashionable. Tell all the men to play golf and ship the women patients off to the West Indies.'

A man got off a train very green in the face. A doctor friend met him and asked him what was wrong. 'Train sickness,' he said. 'I always get deathly sick when I travel backwards on the train.'

'Why didn't you ask the man sitting opposite to change seats with you?' suggested the doctor.

'I thought of that, but there wasn't anybody there!'

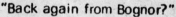

"Back again from Bognor?"

"Did you say you smelt bacon frying last night, Myrtle?"

'There are burglars in the kitchen eating all my pies and cakes. Phone for a policeman quickly.'
'I'll phone for a doctor. They won't need a policeman.'

"Act nonchalant"

"Watch it — here comes the hostess!"

A doleful-looking customer went to the bar and ordered six whiskies. The barman poured them out for him in six glasses. 'Now line them up in front of me, will you?' asked the customer. He then paid for them and told him to keep the change. He swallowed down the contents of the first glass in line and then repeated the process with the third and fifth glasses. Then, saying, 'Goodnight,' he turned to walk away.

'Excuse me,' said the barman. 'You have left three glasses untouched.'

'Yes, I know,' he said. 'The doctor said he didn't mind me taking the odd drink.'

"Do you know, dear, you can see 5 television regions from up here!"

"Well, you should insist they give you your fortnight in summer like everyone else."

"What do I do? . . . pay by the inch?"

"Something real he-manish, Miss —
I don't want geezers gettin'
the wrong idea."

Two old Scotsmen, one a doctor and the other a
dentist for many years, had wondered how old the
other was. However, neither would say. Suddenly
the dentist died, and the doctor knew that if he
peeped into the grave he would at last know, from
the inscribed brass plate, if his friend was older
than he. When the funeral service was over he
leaned over the grave and looked at the brass plate.
It only said: 'Angus McFarley, Surgeon Dentist —
Hours: 10 till 4.'

"Don't tell me! — You've been to that. ruddy antique shop aga . . . "

"Well, don't just SIT there — get an evening job . . . "

"No, Henry, we're NOT home yet — we're still in Harridges!"

"I'm just the same, can't manage to save a penny these days!"

"It's too expensive — I'll wait until you have your sale.

The pretty nurse tried to comfort the newly arrived patient by saying: 'Don't let the doctors frighten you. Doctors are like politicians — they view with alarm so they can point with pride.'

"Johnson, you're yawning!"

"Still — it keeps them from hanging around the streets."

"I've told you before . . . those are MY collars."

"I've heard his congregation is dwindling, but this is ridiculous!"

"For goodness sake, Alfred — nobody's trying to look at your cards!"

"I came away with a small fortune today — trouble is, I started with a BIG one!"

"Hey, Boss — that bloke with the computer's here again!"

"Well, it isn't the way we used to play happy families at home, Mr. Grabbles!"

"All right — you beat him at snap!"

"Hullo — another cutback in defence spending?"

"I expect you'd like to sit with your mates . . ."

"This is the short-cut I told you about, Dave."

OPTICIAN

"Careful, Marjoribanks! — Do you realise the price of oxygen?"

"No, matron — in the lapel!"

"As far as I can make out from this prescription, you're suffering from potato blight!"

"Those were her very words doctor — 'My feet are killing me'!"

"Don't worry about his loss of memory, doctor, it wasn't a very good one."

"If you can't be a good loser, don't play!"

"She'll do anything to scrape an acquaintance!"

"Smithy's certainly gambling the lot on this hand!"

A man said to his doctor, 'I think there's something the matter with me; I've got a pain here, one there, one over here . . .' he went on and on about his symptoms.

Every time he paused for breath the doctor said, 'Fine! Fine! Go on, go on!'

When he'd finally finished the story the doctor said, 'You know, you've got a disease that was supposed to have been extinct long ago.'

Specialisation in medicine has gone too far in the opinion of some of the older doctors. One of them was talking to a medical student who said, 'When you graduate I suppose you're going to be a specialist like so many of the young men nowadays?'

'Yes, doctor,' he replied, 'I'm going to specialise in diseases of the nose.'

'Indeed?' the older man snorted. 'Which nostril?'

"Isn't it about time you got used to this 'phone ringing, Ethel?"

"I think you had better let them pin their own flags on!"

"Be rather interesting to know if our insurance covers us against this sort of thing!"

"B!"

OPTICIAN

"Sounds as if we've caught that ruddy mouse at last."

Two patients in an asylum met one day. 'I'll bet you ten pence you don't know what I've got in my hand,' said the first.

'A helicopter,' said the second.

The first looked cautiously through his fingers and said, 'No, guess again.'

'A rowing boat then?' he said.

'No,' came the reply, 'guess again.'

'A cow?' he asked.

'What colour?'

'Black,' he said, 'so pay me ten pence.'

'It's not fair,' said the first, 'you looked.'

"I'm a T.V. interviewer and . . . "

"He was here first!"

"Mother's very upset. She paid ten bob a pound for those mushrooms."

An old Scotsman's wife was nearing her end and the family were gathered at the bedside. At last she made a sign that she wanted to speak to her husband. She said weakly: 'I realise that you dinna like my sister Janet, but I want you to let her ride beside you in the first carriage at my funeral.'

Her husband was very much affected, but at last was able to answer: 'Well, Maggie, I'll do it for you, but mind you, it'll spoil my day.'

'A new elixir will make a man live for 200 years.'

'If I were a bachelor I'd buy a bottle.'

"I bought him at the
Army Surplus store!"

"Couldn't we leave it till
tomorrow? It's raining
cats and dogs!"

"Don't join any walkouts
for the next two weeks."

"Just giving him his nose drops, doctor."

"In THIS hospital, nurse, we like to use more modern
methods of inducing sleep!"

"Another blinkin' letter from St. Paul to the Corinthians!"

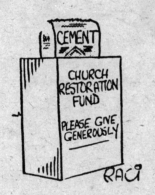

"Big service today, Forbes Check organ pressure . . . adjust lectern . . . top-up font . . . "

' . . . As the actress said to the Bishop . . . "

"... and when I finally managed to explain the gravity of the export problem, I'm afraid your daughter just fainted right away ...."

"Sis! It's the one who can do every bird imitation — except migrate."

"Of course I'll have to get his permission — he's my husband."

The lady dashed into the office, as she had decided that she simply *must* see a doctor. She cried: 'I feel terrible! You must tell me what's wrong with me, and don't spare my feelings either.'

He said: 'Well, let's have a look at you,' and gave her a thorough examination. Then he said, 'Well, I've got three things to say to you. Firstly you are too fat, secondly you are terribly neurotic and thirdly I'm the window cleaner — Doctor Woodhouse is on the next floor up!'

Two specialists were on holiday and were watching the passers by as they sipped their drinks at a pavement café. One, an orthopaedic surgeon, said: 'These young girls here have lovely legs, don't you think? Most beautiful I've seen in all my experience.'

The other shrugged and said: 'I didn't notice, I'm a chest man myself.'

"But I hardly scratched the paintwork."

A doctor tells of a young man who came to him because of pains in his head and at times confused in his thinking. The doctor asked him if his nurse had ever dropped him on his head when he was a baby.

'Oh, no,' said the young man, 'we couldn't afford a nurse. My mother used to do it!'

"Did you know that all the rain we've had has made the garage shrink?"

"You'll never guess — the policeman who booked me was the living image of Sean Connery."

"Right — now forward a little."

"Nothing much today, doctor — two Napoleons, one pink elephant, and a 'Nobody loves me'."

"This dream world you live in, Mr. Morton — how about taking me back there with you!"

"Now you say you have the feeling that everybody's staring at you."

"My feeling of failure started when I was a Boy Scout — a poor old lady I was helping across the road got run over."

'Mind giving this parcel to
the chap next door?
He's having a bath!'

"That mirror, Henry? I got it at
a jumble sale — why?"

"Don't make such a fuss, dear,
you're not the first man to cut
himself shaving!"

Doctor: 'There's no need to worry about your
wife; you'll have a different woman when she
gets back from the hospital.'
   Anxious husband: 'And what if she finds
out?'

"How much longer are you going to be in there!"

"If the men don't get satisfaction,
they're liable to turn ugly!"

"Nice bit of lagging—
what a pity it's scaffolding."

'Doctor!' called Mr Cohen frantically. 'Come quick! You know my wife always sleeps with her mouth wide open? Well, a mouse ran down her throat!'

The doctor said: 'I'll be over in a few minutes, meanwhile try waving a piece of cheese in front of her mouth and maybe the mouse will pop out.'

When the doctor reached Cohen's house he found Mr Cohen in his shirt sleeves waving a six pound flounder in front of the woman's face. 'What's the idea?' asked the doctor. 'I told you to use a piece of cheese — mice don't like flounders.'

'I know, I know,' gasped Cohen, 'but we've got to get the cat out first.'

"I distinctly said NO mustard! . . . Now
get back there and tell him . . ."

"The days don't drag so since I had the radio fitted."

"There she goes . . . driving him to drink again!"

"It's your own damn fault . . . I was taught to drive by your school!"

"Money can't buy happiness, but at least it would buy automatic transmission!"

'You and your 'Special Offer Honey-Boy After-shave Lotion' . . . !"

A man was ruining his health by drinking far too much, and his doctor told him that he simply had to cut down his drinking by half. The man promised. The doctor saw him a few weeks later. The man smelled of alcohol, but he swore that he'd cut his drinking by half.

Later the doctor was called to the man's home as he was in a very bad way. 'You swore that you had cut your drinking down by half,' he said to the patient.

'I did, doctor,' the man said weakly, 'I haven't had a chaser since I last saw you!'

"Goodbye Carstairs — and good luck!"

"M.I.5. Disguise Department — Miss Wilkinson speaking."

"It's my private eye."

"Fancy some microfilms for afters, Boris?"

"It's not their fault, officer — my stuff is very controversial."

"Brilliant, my boy! May I buy it?"

"Yes, I love it, I LOVE it — but where are the clues?"

"Most of his friends have gone commercial, but not my Arthur!"

"Now, Miss Gooseflesh you remember the pose you took yesterday . . . ?"

"Remember, Fred, when we used to gaze into each other's eyes on the beach like that?"

" . . . and that's my poor, dear wife again. Naturally, I thought that Thing was only after her ice-cream cornet."

"NOW what do we do for spending money?"

"English economy wing? . . . First on your left!"

"But how can you have blisters already? We've only walked down the garden path."

" . . . and I find I get tired and irritable after an hour in your waiting room!"

"I'm just taking the wife to the doctor — she doesn't seem well at all."

"The new doctor's one of those young, progressive fellows."

"Oh, well — that's show-business."

"I hate to say this — but exhale!"

USED T.V. LOT

"This set's a real bargain . . .
used to belong to a little old
lady with weak eyes . . ."

"A fine time to be called out,
halfway through the night
it's the Doctor again!"

"Tired? Listless? No energy?
What you need is . . ."

"A quantity of dynamite has
been reported missing from
Clinker Colliery. Will anyone . . ."

STUDIO B
BBC SOUND

"I thought this play was
for television!"

"I have no statement to make
your wife and I are just good
friends."

"No, I don't remember snogging in the back row with you when
this film first came out in 1944 — I was in North Africa."

"Are you in a hurry for this?"

"Quick! He's swallowed a microphone."

"If you're looking for his chest,
it's slipped farther down the bed."

"I'm sorry, we can't accept any more of
your blood, your last pint bounced."

"Don't tell ME there's nothing wrong with me. I was in failing health
before you were born."

"There's another ten minutes to knocking-off time, Johnson."

"Don't worry, sir, — your wife can't make up her mind what colour she wants the ceiling!"

"Very nice indeed, Hornsby The only snag is this happens to be a glove factory!"

"I see, sir — oyster lustre ceiling and emerald mist walls. Fred, fetch a tin of white and a tin of green."

"All that fuss because it's the wrong way up."

"The next programme comes via Early Bird and Eurovision links, especially for you."

"There goes the last one, Charlie — may as well play 'The Queen'."

"Don't they ever change the programme? It's been just like this ever since we bought the set."

"Albert! They distinctly asked you not to adjust the set."

"I think this tough interviewing business is getting out of hand."

"By gum, there'll be some phone calls about THIS!"

"Is this a live programme?"

"Notice how that new bloke is sucking up to the Foreman?"

"If you don't watch out, the blokes'll begin to notice there's 'somefing between you and that canteen bit."

"I just got the sack!"

"It's his half-day."

"How did YOU think we made the holes in colanders, then?"

"That's odd, Your Royal Highness
— I felt sure he'd stop."

then the wife suggested
entering this petrol competition
and, well, here we are!"

"I gave strict orders that the
Mayor's Parade was for local
shopkeepers only!"

"It's just what I wanted!"

"Hm! No underfelt!"

"No no, James — the poisoned
soup is for His Excellency!"

"Thank God you stopped him officer, he's been cutting me up all along the road."

"Well, I think YOUR optician ought to have HIS eyes tested!"

"My word — but for your very prompt action in slamming on the brakes — we might have run over that little dicky bird!"

"I'm only firing on 143 cylinders."

"Act nonchalant."

"Exactly what they forecast on T V."

"First, a word about last night's hurricane."

"You read the weather forecast fine, Smith — it's just that they didn't like the adjectives you used!"

"I'm sick of getting drenched!"

"Ar! You should have had 'em lagged mate!"

"That's right — make the ashtray untidy!"

"Thought so! — You didn't wipe your feet!"

"You never buy ME any ants's eggs, do you?"

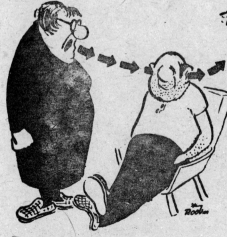

"I want something feminine and dainty, yet capable of a good, sharp kick."

"Let's face it, Smith, as a projectionist you're a flop!"

"It comes out all right in the end — he shoots her."

"Take us in, mister?"

"What's it like?"

"One single at 2/9d."

"Hang on a sec, Jim — you get a simply wonderful stereo effect from the middle of these one-and-nines"

"Letter for ya, dear, by Pony Express."

"Aw, give the postman his durned Christmas box and let's have done wi' all this!"

The nurse picked up the phone on the fifth floor of the hospital and a voice said: 'Good evening, can you tell me how Mr Sherman is feeling? He's a patient in room 602.'

'Just a minute,' she said, 'I'm not his nurse but I'll be happy to tell you after I look at his chart.'

After looking at the chart she said: 'I'm happy to tell you that Mr Sherman is improving and will be able to leave here in a couple of days.'

'Many thanks to you, so glad to hear the good news,' said the voice.

'Whom shall I say called?' asked the nurse.

'This *is* Mr Sherman!' said the voice. 'The doctors won't tell me a damn thing!'

"Same thing every Sunday mornin' — play-by-play descriptions o' Saturday's gunfights."

"Greetings! — And next time kindly dispense with the twenty arrow salute."

"You don't know this driver like I do!"

"That's mine — I can smell my cheese sandwiches!"

"Did you hear that? — It sounded just like a gunshot."

"You'll never get away with it."

"Oh, and the new lodger sends his regards!"

"I've a feeling somebody grassed!"

"Betty and Fred got married last week, and you're invited to their fiftieth wedding anniversary!"

"In all the years I've stood out there, this is the first time that anyone has ever asked me in!"

"Ah, well — time I was off to the pub . . . ".

"How about Rachmaninoff's Prelude in C Sharp Minor?"

"Psst, Fred! Thanks for the 'Hullo, George, long time no see!' when we came in."

OFF LICENCE

"'ou all 'eard what that chap said. Gimme some brandy."

"Ever wondered why our marriage is a success, Liz? It's 'cos we've got the same interests."

"TIS II — Your lonely vigil is ended!"

"That's Mr. Dobson, my boss."

"I was going to say you'd got him out late — I didn't know you were taking the empties back!"

"Coming in at this time of night — don't you know it's nearly October?"

"Well, how are things with you then, Taff?"

"Captain! The swimming pool is leaking!"

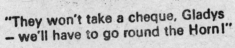

"They won't take a cheque, Gladys — we'll have to go round the Horn!"

"Looks like mutiny, sir."

SEESIK CRUISES
(TOURIST CLASS)

"I know it's mink but why do you always have to buy me something USEFUL?"

" . . . dearer materials . . . extra labour-charges . . ."

"You have it on back to front — oh, I don't know though."

Repairs WHILE-U-WAIT

"I know just what you're going to say, sir, and I agree with you. The buttons need moving!"

"Do you really think it's just a harmless phase he's going through?"

"... and he'll NEVER apologise first — it's ME who has to do the patching-up."

"My husband's carrying on with your wife!"

"Of course there will be some dinner for you if you come around, Mother."

"We've been married a year now, Alice, isn't it about time your Ma stopped crying?"

"Oy, Not so fast — there's still something of yours in the bathroom."

"Pa, can I stop annoying granny, now? — I'm getting tired!"

" . . . Your mother!"

"Don't be silly, mother dear, George and I LOVE having you."

"Shortage of women doesn't seem ta bother old
Tumbleweed none!"

"Eat yore cereal, if ya want ta
grow up fast on the draw like
yore Paw."

"Took a thorn outa his foot once
— now he won't leave me!"

"O' course — ah'll admit it
ain't one of the
quietest neighbourhoods
in the world."

NATIONAL ASSISTANCE BOARD

"I don't know how we managed when my hubby was working."

"You're an anonymous donor, I suppose?"

"SOMEONE here owes the petty cash five bob!"

"Mind you pay the electric bill today."

"Every week Henry puts a little by for next year's rates!"

The doctor saw old McTavish walking along leaning heavily on a very short stick. 'Hello there, Sandy,' said the doctor. 'Is that rheumatism troubling you again?' 'No, doctor, I broke ma stick!'

"I — er — just called to wish you good morning!"

"Your wages got frozen."

"Well, dear, we've finally saved enough coupons to send away for an ashtray — gimme a couple of quid to post 'em."

"In aid of the Tin-Collection-Box-makers' Benevolent Fund, ma'am."

"Gentlemen of the jury, have you reached a verdict?"

A stockbroker who had undergone a medical examination for a life insurance policy, received a telegram: 'Regret to inform you – your tests show you have pneumonia, heart disease and a stomach ulcer. An hour later another telegram arrived. It said: 'Sorry – first telegram – mistake. Confused your test with another patient.' The patient sent back the following reply: 'Too late – have already committed suicide.'

"Then his lordship said 'So you have no fixed abode? – We can soon fix THAT!'"

"I got on great, the judge gave me twelve months in Holloway."

"Here, take my card in case you need me again some time!"

"You're not helping your case by addressing me as 'Madam Chairman'!"

"We find the defendant just a teeny-weeny bit guilty!"

"May I have ten bob to tide me over until you're in a better mood?"

STATION ANNOUNCEMENTS TRANSLATED ONLY 5/-

"Jack Lilburn, I never thought you'd go through with this!"

"Now which of you did he know as 'Pussykins'?"

'Your left leg is swollen but I shouldn't worry about it too much.'

'No,' said the patient, 'and if *your* left leg was swollen I wouldn't worry too much about it either.'

"I'm just about fed up with staying in while you read my endowment policies and bank statements, Fiona . . ."

The old boozer had to see his doctor about his condition. 'You know, your problem is that you drink far too much. It'll be the death of you, I'm warning you!' said the doctor, and with that he pulled out a bottle from the man's pocket.

'What's this?' he exclaimed. 'Why you even have the nerve to bring drink into my surgery!'

Quick as a flash the boozer said: 'Oh, that, sir . . . well, you see, sir, I've just come back from a holiday in Lourdes and that is . . . er . . . a bottle of the Holy Water.'

The doctor pulled out the cork and took a sip of the contents. 'Great heavens!' he said, 'this is gin!'

'Glory be to God!' said the man. 'Another miracle!'

"But Mr. Pugh, I always thought lifeboat practice was on deck with everybody there."

"I've told him we're eighty thousand tons and we're still in the port, but all he says is: 'Better be safe than sorry' "

"Back, I say — BACK you mutinous dogs!"

"You need double top for game, Bert!"

"You're wasting your time, they're probably all watching a film!"

"Sorry, everyone — false alarm!"

"And whose bright idea was it to build a sunken bath?"

NOISE ABATEMENT SOCIETY

"If you ask me, she's getting too big for her boots!"

"This bit here, where the punk puts the bite on the D.A., is YUMMY!"

"I have a question. Do you want cheese or sardines for supper, dear?"

"I say, your Grandfather IS a slow reader, isn't he?"

"Produce 25 Merry Mop Meat Pies and recite the soliloquy from Hamlet and you win ten bob."

"He's wasting his breath — it's closed on Sundays."

"Don't look now, Miss Wilson, but I fear we have a troublemaker on our hands."

"Lovely! You can't beat a nice, old-fashioned imitation log fire!"

"I think they must be putting something in our tea . . ."

"I hate these sad endings, don't you?"

"I say, Ferguson, wouldn't these make wonderful sleeping bags?"

"About the ventilator you've just fitted . . . "

"What are you staring at? Clear off!"

"You've been chatting up a tent for the last half-hour!"

"Fisby, would you kindly remove those ridiculous transfers?"

"For goodness' sake make up your mind whether or not you want to grow a beard and let's get to bed!"

Doctor: (To extremely fat lady): 'Look, I'm going to give you a diet and some slimming pills. I would like half of you to return in two months time for a check up.'

The doctor was very worried as Mrs Burgess didn't appear to be making very good progress after her operation, and she had little will to get better. On visiting day, the doctor had a few words with the patient's husband, who was anxious as his wife had been away now for several weeks. Two days later Mrs Burgess was making rapid progress — a complete change for the better! She had received a letter from her husband, which had said: 'Don't worry, darling, I'm managing very nicely. Two or three girls from the office come in to help with the housework . . .'

"Left or right?"

"I still think a mini-skirt getting out of a mini-car is far more breathtaking."

"Er, I'm the 'other man'."

PROFESSORS ANNUAL CONFERENCE.

"Hey, Mac, is the moon like out then?"

"You're not going out again, are you, Franz?"

"It's ages since we had one of these unsliced loaves."

"When does your pen-pal go home?"

"When's blast-off time?"

"Oh, dear, don't tell me I've forgotten to sugar the rhubarb tart again."

"Let's have a freak-out."

"Bless you!"

"I TOLD you I wasn't very photogenic."

"Dear Poison-pen pal . . . "

"I think you're spoiling that dog."

"Go on behaving like this and you'll be sent down!"

"Take him for a proper walk — no wonder the poor thing's neurotic!"

"When I bought him you said he was fully grown!"

"Hide, you idiot, we're supposed to be extinct!"

"He's doing his best to help me get over poor Fido passing on."

"You'll never guess what I had for lunch today."

"Never mind, dear, I think you're beautiful."

"Nigel! You PROMISED me you'd lay off the dog pills!"

"I'm glad MY husband doesn't do that every morning — she's their maid."

"How do you know you don't like it? You've never had chips and custard before."

"I really must fit that serving hatch with a sliding door!"

"We're worried about Cynthia. So far no Lord Right has turned up."

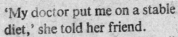

'My doctor put me on a stable diet,' she told her friend.
  'Don't you mean a staple diet?'
  'No,' she said, 'Stable diet – I'm on oats and hay three times a day.'

" 'Er Grace says 'Belt up'!"

"Arnold, do you realise your soup is getting cold?"

"I've just had an argument with the gardener, dear!"

Asylum. A man entered the principal's office and said, 'I would have been here a little sooner had I not come quite so late. I left orders at the hotel to be called early in the morning, but they made a mistake and woke up the wrong man, consequently I was half way here before I discovered I was not the man, so I had to go back and wake myself up.'

"With a face like that, it's about time you learned to say something besides 'Pretty Polly'."

"It's cruel the way they coop those poor humans up."

"If I didn't bring him with me, he wouldn't let me back in."

"What a lovely dog. Where does he live?"

"Let us imagine Inspector Maggs is a cat stuck up a tree."

"Calm down, dear. There's a perfectly simple explanation. . . ."

"Would you be terribly, awfully angry if I changed my mind and didn't go after all?"

"It's your last chance, Elaine — if anything happens to THIS one, we'll have to put you on to making the tea!"

"Met Arnold through a marriage bureau they'd only just started up, so there wasn't much choice."

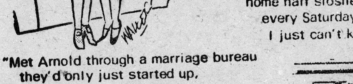

"Out drinking till all hours — coming home half sloshed — football every Saturday — always broke — I just can't keep up with her!"

"Right, Mr. Kamasuki, seventy gross 'I'm Backing Britain' ties, thirty gross 'I'm Backing Britain', hankies, and twelve thousand 'I'm Backing Britain' pens, delivery next week."

"What do you mean you're a 'Don't know'? — I haven't asked you anything yet!"

The young doctor approached the pretty young nurse and said: 'I see that Mr Williams isn't chasing you any more, nurse. How did you put a stop to that?'

'Easy,' she said, 'I simply took the tyres off his wheelchair!'

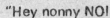

"Hey nonny NO!

"He wasn't very good at Postman's Knock. . . ."

"My husband came down half an hour ago to complain about the noise . . ."

Doctor (to young girl, prior to examination): 'Now don't get nervous, Miss. Just get a hold of yourself. Better still I'll do it for you!'

"Here's someone to listen to you."

"If I had married Fred Barnsley,
HE'D have taken me somewhere
for holidays."

"What's for breakfast, Ethel?"

While in Hollywood a businessman had to be given a blood transfusion as he had had a car accident. As it transpired he was given the blood of actor Dean Martin. They pumped three pints of blood into him and when he awoke he gave the nurse three choruses of 'Nellie Dean!'

The idiot went to get a box of sleeping pills from his chemist from a prescription his doctor had given him. He asked the chemist, 'Are they male sleeping pills or female sleeping pills?'
    The chemist said: 'What difference does it make?'
    'A great deal. How do I know whether to put them in pyjamas or a nightdress?'

"He can't get used to a bungalow
— every time it rains we get this
performance!"

"Molly! How many kids have we now?"

"You're spoiling that dog, Joe."

"Is it ALWAYS lovely wet weather like this, Mum?"

"That's the last time I give you dancing lessons!"

"Are you going to get in or do I have to throw you in?"

"He always likes to keep the children amused in some way"

"Am I to understand you disagree with me?"

"You appear to have upset your drink, sir. Will you permit me to purchase you another?"

"I'd rather YOU told him to stop insulting you, dear you know what a nasty temper I've got."

"Well . . . what do YOU want?"

"Sir, despite our contrasting opinions, I'm convinced that a combined effort will enable us to reach some measure of warm agreement — to our mutual benefit."

"Steady! It's considered very dangerous to strike a chemist with a bottle of nitroglycerin in his pocket!"

"Old J.B. can be pretty rough if your sales are below target."

"Sounds like Doreen — no doubt with some fantastic excuse for being late again."

"Just had Chobley in here. Asked for a rise and when I said NO, he fell grovelling at my feet."

"I've been expecting you!

"Miss Jones — why is it I always get the broken biscuits and the cup with a chip in it?"

HEAD BUYER

'Doctor, if this swelling gets any bigger on my leg, I won't be able to get my trousers on!'
  'Here take this.'
  'What is it?'
  'The address of a nudist colony!'

"I knew it! They've charged for the baby again!"

'ee . . . something tempting, with a hint of moonlight and roses."

"Isn t that the chap who told us he was a liver and kidney specialist?"

"It couldn't be much fresher, madam, I only ran over it this morning."

"What a marvellous offer, Dudley remind me to buy a dog on the way home!"

"Fired? I always thought slaves were sold!"

"Be sure you're not working when he arrives, then he'll think I'm out!"

"Sir — ninety three point five per cent of our staff want more money."

"I can never tell whether Dobson is overworked, too slow, or absent."

"Don't overdo it, Fanshaw, there's still the other foot."

"Oh, hello, darling . . . OF COURSE I still love you. I always will . . . What? Oh, nothing much . . . just taking some dictation . . ."

"He is pleased to see you!"

"I suggest you take a couple of weeks off, Miss Jones — I think the work is beginning to tell on you!"

"Get me Perry Mason!"

"I think I preferred it when we had mice."

"We'll have to find another excuse to meet secretly."

"If you don't get off, I won't let you watch the dog-food commercials!"

"That insurance policy's a real bargain — you ought to break your leg more often!"

"I can picture you now, sir, breakfast in bed every morning!"

"Can I hear this one, please?"

"Now what else is there? Oh, yes, dog biscuits."

'The doctor's here, sir.'
Absent-minded man: 'I can't see him. Tell him I'm ill!'

"Just popping out for fags, love.

"I suppose when I get a job you'll forget me and these stolen moments together .."

"What else can you do besides reign?"

"Actually we get very few demands for a vandal."

"No, it doesn't look as though I've got a vacancy for a mercenary at the moment."

"I tell you it isn't EVERY man who's replaced by an electronic brain!"

" 'Ow abaht formin' a group?"

"Why don't we just buy a mousetrap?"

"Think yer'll be discovered by next week, son? 'Cos that's when the electricity bill's duel"

"Smile, please!"

"I think he wants a tip."

" . . . and try not to cause another run on Sterling."

" . . . and if you put the policy in your wives' names, on your death, they will each receive 39s. 4d . . . "

. . . a quarter of assorted diamonds please."

SCHOOL FOR SNAKE CHARMERS

"People like that are a constant drain on the National Health."

"I'd like to report my wife missing — as from tomorrow."

"Ah! It's how he'd have wanted to go!"

"I knew you'd soon come creeping back to apologise!"

'You're planning to go to Vienna? But that will cost you a fortune.'

'Oh, not really. You see, I'll have my youth restored by Dr Steinach and come back on a child's ticket.'

"What's happened to everybody?"

"Trust YOU not to notice that I vacuumed the inside of the car for you, today!"

"No, that's reverse!"

"Sister Veronica! — Remember your vows of humility . . . !"

'You must be very careful and follow the right instructions for taking this pill,' said the chemist.

Murphy: 'Go on with yer! There's only one direction for it to go.'

"Dad! . . . Mum's devalued our car again."

"Shteady, dear! . . . Mind that Posht! . . . Watch out for . . ."

Hurry up, Helen — I can't hold on much longer!"

"How do you spell 'Chapter One'?"

"It's a recipe a friend gave me for making husbands take their wives out to dinner."

"He just threw me some nuts."

"Now, what's a nice girl like you doing in a place like this?"

"Going over a cliff wasn't bad enough, oh, no — YOU have to land on a submarine."

'Our dog bit the mother-in-law today so I've just taken him to the vet.'
   'To get him destroyed?'
   'No to get his teeth sharpened.'

"Don't forget your tool kit, sir!"

"Could I please have a word with someone about after-sales service?"

A doctor was passing a stonemason's yard and called out: 'Morning, Mr Smith! Hard at work, I see. I notice that you finish your gravestone as far as, "In memory of" — and then wait, I presume, to see who the monument is intended for?'
   'Why, yes,' the mason replied. 'Unless, of course, somebody's sick and *you* attend him, and then I keep straight on!'

"I'm dreading Christmas — last year they ALL gave me after-shave lotion!"

"This sort of thing's going to KILL us small shopkeepers!"

"Now this is one of our more interesting stock-taking jobs."

"Like to come out for an English meal tonight?"

" — and stop disappearing when I'm talking to you!"